LET'S LEARN ABOUT...

THE SKY

PROJECT BOOK

CBEEBIES

K3

P **Pearson**

Pearson Education Limited
KAO Two, KAO Park, Harlow, Essex, CM17 9NA, England
and Associated Companies around the world

First published 2020

ISBN: 978-1-292-33459-2

Set in Mundo Sans
Printed in China SWTC/01

Acknowledgements
The publishers and author(s) would like to thank the following people and institutions for their feedback and comments during the development of the material: Marcos Mendonça, Leandra Dias, Viviane Kirmeliene, Simara H. Dal'Alba, Mônica Bicalho and GB Editorial. The publishers would also like to thank all the teachers who contributed to the develoment of *Let's learn about...*:
Adriano de Paula Souza, Aline Ramos Teixeira Santo, Aline Vitor Rodrigues Pina Pereira, Ana Paula Gomez Montero, Anna Flávia Feitosa Passos, Camila Jarola, Celiane Junker Silva, Edegar França Junior, Fabiana Reis Yoshio, Fernanda de Souza Thomaz, Luana da Silva, Michael Iacovino Luidvinavicius, Munique Dias de Melo, Priscila Rossatti Duval Ferreira Neves, Sandra Ferito and all the schools that took part in Construindo Juntos.

Author Acknowledgements
Rhiannon S. Ball

Image Credit(s):
BBC Worldwide Learning: 5, 7, 9, 13, 15, 19, 23, 27, 25, 31, 33, 35; **Pearson Education Ltd:** Silva Serviços de Educação 5, 5, 5, 5, 7, 11, 13, 15, 15, 15, 19, 21, 25, 29, 29, 29, 29, 31, 33, 35, 51, 51, 51, 51, 51, 53, 53; **Shutterstock. com:** AnnstasAg 21, Benchart 23, Ghrzuzudu 33, Klara Viskova 17, Ksenya Savva 17, NotionPic 27, Saraoom Design 9, uhammad Desta Laksana 33, Virinaflora 33, Yayayoyo 33, Yusufdemirci 21

Illustration Acknowledgements
Illustrated by Filipe Laurentino and Silva Serviços de Educação.

Cover illustration © Filipe Laurentino

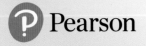

CONTENTS

LOOK AND THINK. COMPLETE AND COLOR.

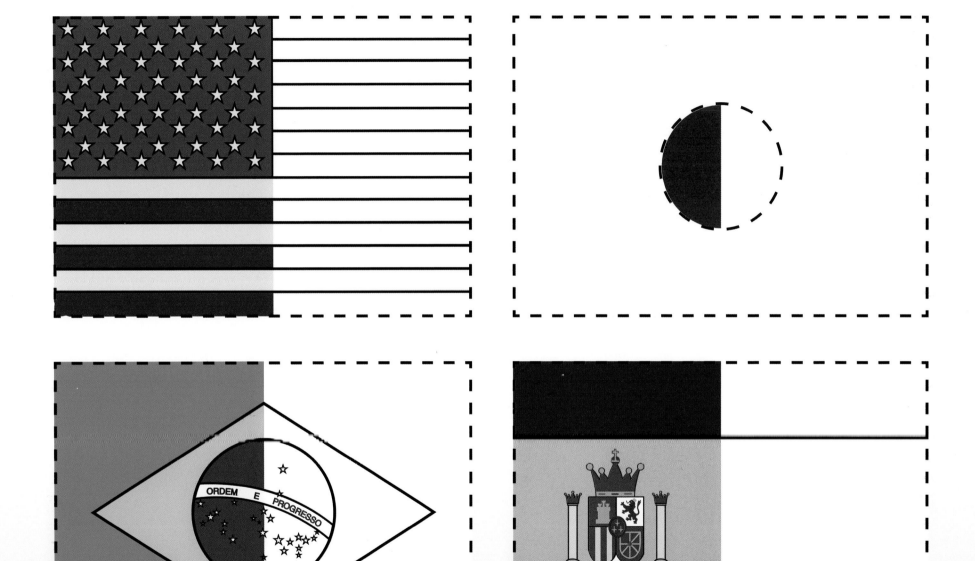

LOOK, FIND, STICK, AND DRAW.

LOOK, THINK, AND DRAW.

LOOK, DRAW, AND COLOR.

LOOK, THINK, AND STICK.

LOOK, THINK, CIRCLE, AND COLOR.

LOOK AND FOLLOW. COLOR.

LOOK, THINK, AND CIRCLE.

LOOK , THINK, AND FIND. COLOR.

MAKE A CITY PARK. DRAW AND COLOR.

LOOK AND COLOR. THINK AND STICK.

LOOK, THINK, AND DRAW.

LOOK, THINK, AND MATCH. COLOR.

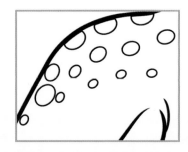 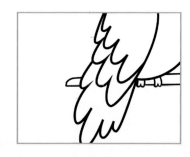  

LOOK, THINK, MATCH, AND DRAW.

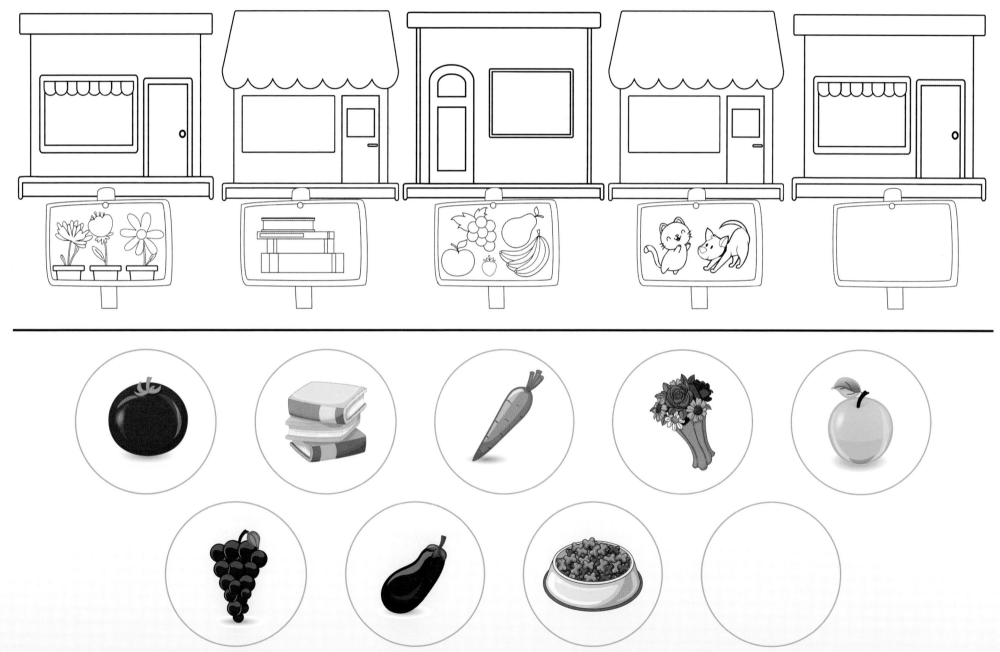

LOOK, GLUE, AND DRAW.

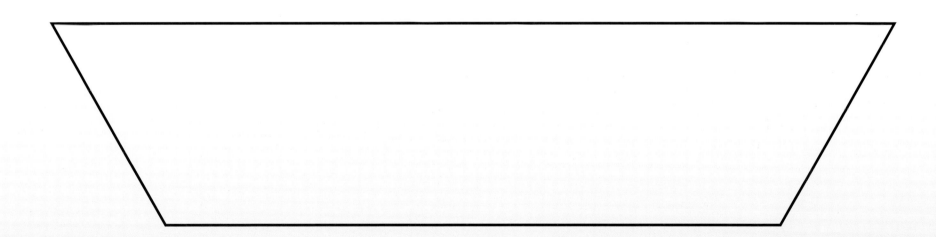

DRAWING

DRAW.

DRAW.

DRAW.

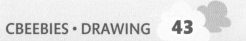

DRAW.

STICKERS

STICKERS

UNIT 1

UNIT 3

STICKERS

UNIT 6

UNIT 7